Original title:
Lost in a Blizzard (Again)

Copyright © 2024 Creative Arts Management OÜ
All rights reserved.

Author: Dean Whitmore
ISBN HARDBACK: 978-9916-94-286-4
ISBN PAPERBACK: 978-9916-94-287-1

A Labyrinth of Cold Comfort

Socks mismatched, I brave the freeze,
My nose red, and bubbling knees.
I chase a snowman, he runs away,
"What's the hurry?" I shout play.

Snowflakes tickle, pants all wet,
Puppy laughs, oh what a pet!
Fumbling mittens, I lose my grip,
Time for cocoa, let's take a sip.

The Veiled Pathway of Snow

My boots squelch, what a sight,
Snow drifts dancing, pure delight.
I fall flat, a flurry in tow,
Careful now, don't let it show.

A snowball flies from nowhere fast,
Hit my head, oh what a blast.
With frozen fingers, I laugh aloud,
Join the chaos, a frosted crowd.

Serenity Caught in the Storm

Whirls and twirls, a scenic mess,
A sledding snail, oh what finesse!
Teach me your ways, you little friend,
Carving tracks, this fun won't end.

My scarf's a tangle, my cheeks are pink,
I wave to a snowman, he won't blink.
Upon this hill, I roll and slide,
With giggles snorting, let joy collide.

The Ethereal Drift of Solitude

In fluffy gaps, I stumble wide,
A winter wonderland, one joyous ride.
Through fluffy clouds, I sing a tune,
Where's my hat? It flew to the moon!

My tea gets cold, but that's alright,
Who needs warmth in snowy flight?
With every flake, I seize the cheer,
This frosty game, I hold so dear.

Tales from the Eye of the Storm

A snowman wobbles, then falls down,
He wears a hat, but it's a frown.
The snowflakes dance in a goofy craze,
I trip and tumble in winter's maze.

The wind it howls, a playful tease,
I'm battling snow like a movie freeze.
A penguin bobbles past with flair,
I wave hello, but he doesn't care.

Where Footprints Fade

My boots are lost, or so it seems,
They've wandered off to snowy dreams.
Each print I make just disappears,
I hope they're off to grab some beers.

The snowdrifts whisper, secrets shared,
Where did I go? No one has stared.
With snowballs flying, laughter loud,
I wonder why I'm lost in a crowd.

Vanishing into the White Haze

A squirrel skates, I take a peek,
He looks so fancy, I feel so weak.
I slip on ice, it's quite the sight,
And tumble down without a fight.

The blizzard roars, a wild drum,
I grab my gloves, they're feeling glum.
In all the chaos, I see a cat,
He's building snowmen, imagine that!

Captured by the Snowfall

The flakes like feathers fall from the sky,
I try to catch them, oh my, oh my!
They tickle my nose, then disappear,
Why is this weather so full of cheer?

A snowball fight turns into a splash,
I'm dodging snow like a daring smash.
The world's a mess, but oh what fun,
When winter's games leave everyone stunned!

A Path Obscured by Flurries

White clouds dance above my head,
With each gust, I feel misled.
Footprints vanish, then appear,
I chase my tail, it's all unclear.

Snowflakes tickle my frozen nose,
I spin around, then suddenly froze.
A snowman laughs, it seems he knows,
That winter's game is filled with woes.

Ghosts of Warmth in the Chill

I wear my hat almost like a crown,
My nose, a cherry, it won't live down.
Sipping cocoa, I spill a bit,
The marshmallows flee, oh what a hit!

Footsteps hidden beneath the snow,
The warmth inside feels like a show.
I talk to myself, and what a delight,
Only to find I'm quite the sight!

The Silence of the Snowbound

In this hush, I start to sing,
The snowflakes join, it's quite the thing.
I trip on ice, oh what a sight,
The snowmen giggle, their laughter bright.

Wandering herbs, I seek for green,
But all I find is a frosty scene.
My boots are heavy, my cheeks are red,
Yet here I am, happy instead!

Moments Lost in the Whirl

Twirl of snowflakes, a dizzy ride,
A frozen dance, I'm full of pride.
But wait! Is that a snowball fight?
I join the fray with pure delight.

The mistletoe hangs from branches bare,
While snowmen deck the frosty air.
I tumble down, all in good fun,
The blustery day has just begun!

The Cocoon of Cold

Wrapped tight in my puffy coat,
I waddle like a penguin afloat.
My mittens are lost, is it one or two?
Oh wait, there's my foot, is that stuck too?

The snowflakes dance in the chilly air,
I start to sneeze, oh, that's not fair!
A snowman glances with a frosty stare,
As I face-plant hard—now that's a rare pair!

A Symphony of Snow and Silence

Snowflakes whisper a gentle tune,
But I trip over my clumsy shoe.
Sounding like thunder, down I slide,
All dignity lost, I can't even hide.

A dog zooms past, like a furry jet,
While I stumble and curse my cold wet pet.
The world is quiet, my laughter sells,
As I build a snow fort—where's my phone? Oh well!

When the World Turns to White

Everything's covered in a snowy sheet,
I'm ready for fun, not for defeat.
Then I slip on a patch, with a shout I'll glide,
Panic in tow, like a thrill-seeking ride.

The kids are out, they throw their snow,
While I build an igloo, missing the flow.
With hot cocoa spills and marshmallows lost,
Every moment just adds to the frost!

Memories on the Frosted Path

Fingers numb, and cheeks aglow,
I walk the path where the snowflakes blow.
Yet one little slip makes me gasp in fright,
As I tumble down, oh what a sight!

Each step I take is a frosty dance,
My boots are slippery, no second chance.
But laughter echoes across the deep,
In this winter wonderland, my heart does leap!

The Color of Isolation in White

Frozen flakes dance in delight,
My car's a snowman, oh what a sight!
Gloves on my feet, I slip and slide,
Winter's joke, I'm taken for a ride.

Snowflakes fall, soft on my nose,
I wave at strangers, frozen toes.
In a world that's all white, I lose my way,
A snowball fight? Just a game to play!

Emptiness Painted in Frost

The path is gone, with no sign in focus,
My GPS says 'You're in a hocus pocus!'
I build a fort, with a snack on the side,
A kingdom of snow where I can abide.

Snowmen spill secrets, giggling in the cold,
'You think you're lost?' they tease, uncontrolled.
The scenery is grand, but I'm stuck in a loop,
Trapped 'til spring in this frosty soup!

The Serenity of a Frozen Soliloquy

Chirping birds are all tucked away,
While I perform my theatrical play.
With cotton clouds draped snug overhead,
I chat with squirrels, or so it is said.

Each snowflake whispers tales of the chill,
As I try to find my lost winter thrill.
With each misstep, a squishy embrace,
I laugh at the dance of this airy race!

Embers of Hope beneath the Snow

Beneath layers of white, dreams grow bold,
Desire to ski, though my skills are old.
I trip on a mound, flip like a pancake,
The trees are my audience, for goodness' sake!

Yet in this chaos, I find my cheer,
For snow adds magic to what I hold dear.
Wrapped in this winter, laughter's the key,
I'm one with the snow, or maybe the tea!

The Light Within the Frost

Snowflakes dance like clumsy fools,
While I squint through my icy goggles,
My mittens mismatched, a sight to see,
  Is this winter or a madman's spree?

The snowman grins, his carrot a tad,
But I just tripped, oh dear, how sad!
  He chuckles as I tumble down,
In this frost, I'm the biggest clown.

The sun peeks out, a teasing friend,
But clouds roll in, they never end.
A snowball fight with my own self,
  In this frosty chaos, I'm no elf.

I stagger forth, boots a slushy mess,
  Wipe my nose, I must confess.
In the winter white, I find some cheer,
With laughter echoing, I persevere.

Frostbitten Whispers of Dread

Shivering thoughts in the chilly air,
I'm a popsicle; it's not fair!
The wind howls like an angry cat,
My hat flies off—now where's that at?

Icicles dangle, sharp as a knife,
What a thrilling winter life!
Last time I checked, I had quite a plan,
But here I am, as lost as I can!

Frozen cheeks, a vibrant hue,
Who knew fun could turn so blue?
A snowball hits me right in the face,
I dodge the next—it's a deadly race!

I laugh at my footprints, all askew,
A zigzag pattern, what a view!
In this winter wonderland of dread,
I'll keep marching on, though underfed!

Solitude in the Hushed White

Silence wraps the world so tight,
In this snowy maze, I'm quite a sight.
No footsteps follow, just me and my fame,
As I trip over nature—what a shame!

A plow truck grumbles, breaks the peace,
But I'm over here, a clumsy beast.
I wave at squirrels, they look alarmed,
Am I the only one who's disarmed?

Snow angels call—awful yet divine,
My creation rights the frosty line.
A flurry of chill invites me to play,
While I roll and tumble in the white ballet.

In silence thick, I hear the giggles,
Even the shadows dance and wiggle.
With snowflakes swirling, I cannot resist,
In this crisp quiet, I find my bliss.

Muffled Steps on Sacred Ground

Each footprint whispers secrets low,
A comedy of errors in the snow.
I shuffle through, a plump parade,
My jacket flaps; I'm unafraid.

Snow-covered trees wave their limbs,
Their icy branches do little for whims.
I sing to squirrels, they roll their eyes,
In this winter chill, I hold the prize!

Hot cocoa waits, a call so sweet,
But first I must not lose my feet.
Muffin crumbs sprinkle where I tread,
A trail of snacks, is this how I'm fed?

Happiness hides in each frosty breath,
Life's too short for the fear of death.
With each soft crunch, I dance around,
In winter's grip, I feel profound!

Bound but Breathless in the White

Snowflakes dance like little sprites,
Filling my boots and tickling my tights.
I waddle like a penguin in this cold mess,
Chasing my hat, oh what a distress!

Every corner I turn, there's more of the same,
Lost my sense of direction, is it all just a game?
I can't see the trees, or remember the ground,
A snowman's laughter is the only sound.

Snowballs fly, but they bounce off my ear,
I duck and I weave, fueled by winter cheer.
But did I just slip? Oh, yes, it was grand,
Trust me, it's all totally part of the plan!

Now I'm stuck with a snowdrift stuck on my shoe,
Mouth full of flakes, it's an odd winter stew.
But hey, I found peace in this frosty delight,
As I frolic and flounder in the pale white light.

Frost-Kissed Wanderlust

Onward I trudge, with my scarf flying free,
I swear it's a blizzard whispering to me.
But I can't quite discern the route that I cling,
Is that a tree or a flag from an ice king?

Frosty the snowman just winked at my shoe,
Is it strange I'm talking to things made of goo?
Each frozen step is a dance of despair,
But I'll twirl with the snowflakes and shake off the glare.

The wind gives a giggle, a playful little tease,
As I perform acrobatics with such awkward ease.
Lost, but I'm smiling like a child in delight,
In this wintry wonderland, my heart feels so light.

A snowdrift just snickered, oh what a sly foe,
Can someone please tell me where I should go?
I'll scribble a map in this powdery fluff,
With all my wild misadventures, that's more than enough!

Navigating the Winter's Cloak

The world's turned white, like a frosty surprise,
With every step forward, I slip and I rise.
I follow my footprints—but where do they lead?
This wintery maze is a puzzling steed!

Puffing my cheeks like a chipmunk in glee,
I thought I'd explore; how hard could it be?
But my phone's a popsicle, can't call for a ride,
In this fluffy chaos, I'm flailing with pride.

Snowflakes giggle, on my nose they do land,
I'm brewing a fittingly frosty plan,
To embrace this chill like I'm back in a show,
With each clumsy move, I've got winter's glow.

Can you hear that? A snowdrift's merry song,
It's a chorus of laughter; oh, winter feels wrong!
As I navigate life in this frozen delight,
I'm dancing with whimsy—oh what a night!

The Illusion of Warmth within Ice

In the midst of snowflakes, I search for a sign,
Like a penguin in flip-flops; oh, how divine!
I've got thermal layers, but they're not quite enough,
The cold is a trickster, and life's gotten tough.

Huddled by a snowman, I tell him my plight,
His carrot nose chuckles, he's full of insight.
"Just throw up your hands, and embrace this drawl,
For laughter's the remedy when winter's a brawl."

Drifting through snowdrifts that seem oh-so sly,
I slide past the neighbors, all from on high,
With each breath, I puff out a cloud in the air,
Winter's a jester, and it knows how to dare!

So here I am frozen, with laughter in tow,
In a merry old world where the cold winds do blow.
With a heart full of chuckles, I'll brave this cold rue,
Finding warmth in the silliness, winter's debut!

The Thawing Heart of the Storm

Snowflakes dance, they twirl and spin,
A wayward hat gets caught in the din.
I trip on my boots, oh what a sight,
With laughter echoing through the white.

Shovels and sleds, a comical crew,
We build a snowman, but it looks like goo.
A carrot nose with a funny grin,
He topples down, and we all break in.

Gloves stained with cocoa, cheeks all aglow,
We chase after pups who steal the show.
But chasing them too leads to slips and slides,
And soon we're all down, laughter collides.

As the sun breaks through, it starts to fade,
We shake off the snow, our plans never made.
With memories sweet, like candy on ice,
Each moment we share, a joy that's nice.

Windswept Remnants of Yesterday

Frosty mornings, a coffee in hand,
Awkwardly bundled, I try to stand.
A gust of wind sends my scarf on a quest,
It flaps like a flag, I can't help but jest.

Outside the window, the world is a blur,
A flurry of flakes makes my brain start to stir.
I build a small igloo, my fortress of fun,
But a snowball fight? Oh, I'm soon on the run!

A tumble on ice, it's laughter galore,
The neighbors are watching, they'll ask for an encore.
With cheeks red and frozen, we plot our next game,
To see who can slip and still feel no shame.

So here we will gather, friends wrapped in cheer,
With hot cocoa mugs and the warmth of good beer.
For even in chaos, we find our delight,
In the madness of winter, we bask in the white.

The Frost on Forgotten Dreams

Chasing the dog through the thick, fluffy fluff,
I thought I was clever, but life got quite tough.
With three overcoats, and a hat that's askew,
I fumble and fidget, what's a dreamer to do?

Sock-slicking pathways, I slide with a grin,
While frostbitten memories swirl in the din.
Last time I thought I'd just glide through the snow,
But that's how I ended up face-first, oh no!

The world's a white canvas, with giggles and squeals,
My snow angel's crooked, but that's how it feels.
Frosty disasters, I'm learning to cope,
With funny missteps that fuel all my hope.

When warmth returns, these days will fade slow,
But I'll keep the laughter as life's gentle flow.
For each slip and slide is a gift we can keep,
A gallery of giggles, forever to leap.

Fragile Traces of the Past

Snow drifts whisper of ages gone by,
Each flake a reminder of laughter and sigh.
I built a tall tower of frosty delight,
And watched as it crumbled in soft, snowy night.

A tumble off stairs, a soft snowball bump,
I laugh with my friends as we each make a thump.
They say I'm a champion, while eyes roll and tease,
For one funny fall from this slippery freeze.

As dusk starts to settle, we share tales of woe,
Of hot chocolate spilled and the warm by the glow.
With stories so silly, we can hardly breathe,
Each giggle and snort, a wintry reprieve.

So here in the snow, we'll dance and we'll play,
Embracing the chaos of another wild day.
For while frost may bind us, it can't freeze our hearts,
In every collapse, a new journey starts.

Murmurs Beneath the Drifted Snow

Fluffy white whispers abound,
Frosted flakes dance all around.
I tripped on a snooze, oh what a sight,
With snow in my pants, it gave a fright!

Snowmen laugh with carrot grins,
As I tumble down, chaos begins.
My scarf is a flag, waving with glee,
In this winter circus, I'm the marquee!

The dog steals my glove, he's quite the thief,
Making me chase him, what a relief!
Snowballs fly while I aim wide,
Who knew a blizzard could be this snide?

The world's a marshmallow, sugary and bright,
Crafting a memory that feels just right.
I take a deep breath, this chill so grand,
While snowflakes stick to my outstretched hand!

Between the Serene and the Savage

A drifted moat surrounds my chair,
Tea is freezing, oh the despair!
While snowmen plot my swift demise,
In the blare of snow, I hear their lies!

With each stomp, the ice gives a squeak,
As I search for warmth, my clothes feel weak.
I slip and slide upon the ground,
With every tumble, laughter resounds!

The mailbox is a mountain high,
I reach for letters, oh me, oh my!
A wind gust hit, my hat is gone,
Off it sailed, like a silly swan!

Snowflakes land upon my face,
Tickling my nose, what a strange grace.
With quirky grins and rosy cheeks,
I cherish this frost with all its peaks!

A Canvas of Cold Emotions

Canvas smeared with icy flair,
Painting goofy shapes in chilly air.
My snowball's miss—a fluffy boomerang,
Hits the snowman, and oh, how he sang!

The world is a canvas, splattered with white,
Where laughter and shivers delight in the night.
With mittens in pockets, I roam like a king,
In this wintry chaos, joy is the thing!

A penguin slides by, what a sight to behold,
As ice sculptures tell stories, so bold.
They chime in like bells, oh melting surprise,
Yet I'd trade it for sun with the warmth of the skies!

Snowforts are castles, and I am the queen,
With towering walls made of frozen sheen.
As snowflakes fall, I giggle and cheer,
In this frosty frenzy, I've nothing to fear!

Pursuing the Untilled Horizon

Horizon's lost in a frosty haze,
As I navigate this snowy maze.
Footprints are hidden, my map is unclear,
Is that a snowbank, or just my fear?

With each gust of wind, I wobble and sway,
Attempting to frolic in this wintry play.
I call out for help, but only birds tease,
While squirrels chatter, sharing their cheese!

Twirls of flakes spin 'round my head,
This whirling dervish, oh what dread!
The horizon's a joke, it laughs and it sneers,
As I fumble and tumble through frozen veers.

But joy is resilient, like the sun behind,
No matter the chaos, merriment's kind.
So I chase the absurd, my trusty sidekick,
In this frosty romp, life's comedy's slick!

Sailing Through the Snowbound Silence

Oh look, a snowman, made of fluff,
He's got a carrot nose, but no hat, tough!
I sail through drifts that pile and rise,
Wondering how snowflakes disguise my size.

The streetlights flicker, they think it's bright,
As I trip over paws in the darkest night.
Do I look like a seal on an ice floe now?
Or is it just my fashion—hey, look at this brow!

My friends all laugh, they point and tease,
While I try to dance with the winter breeze.
But icy patches mock my best attempts,
As I slide like a penguin, what ramps and temps!

With mittens on hands and boots laced tight,
I charge into white, where it's fluffy and light.
But my visions of glory are buried beneath,
And my antics inspire giggles—what a wreath!

Currents of Crystalline Confusion

The world turned white, oh what a scene,
A frosty wonderland, yet I'm unseen.
I plan to ski but wind plays tricks,
I end up twirling like I'm doing flips.

The dogs all laugh as I tumble and roll,
While I try to whistle, it's more of a troll.
Snowflakes tumble, an icy ballet,
Yet my cold, wet socks now betray my play!

Rumors say there's a shortcut near,
But each step I take amplifies my fear.
With every breath, a cloud of white,
I wonder if I left my sanity light!

The snowmen gather in a silent stare,
"Is this child lost? Shouldn't he beware?"
But with every fall, I giggle and grin,
This frosty escapade is where fun begins!

Fragments of a Frosty Memory

The blizzard rages, the winds howl loud,
I'm dressed for adventure, oh dear, so proud.
With cheeks like cherries and nose like a pear,
I march through the drifts without a care.

Each step feels like a game of hide and seek,
As I sink and bob, all tired and weak.
I flirt with hot chocolate, a promise so sweet,
Yet find myself chasing my runaway feet!

A snowball in hand, oh what a plan,
But it lands on my sister—oh dear, what a slam!
We laugh and we squeal, till cheeks turn bright red,
Who knew winter had such a cozy spread?

Frosty confetti is thrown in the air,
While we dance around without much flair.
Though tempers may flare, it's all in good fun,
In this white wonderland, we'll never be done!

The Dilemma of the Silent Gale

The wind whispers secrets, oh what fun spree,
As I try to build castles made of snow glee.
But every loose flake seems to conspire,
With a purpose to thwart my winter desire!

My shovel's a paddle, my path a wide sea,
I steer through the drifts with it's just me.
The neighbors shake heads, they think it's a game,
But I'm missing the point—oh, winter's so lame!

A snowball fight erupts, we laugh and we cheer,
But my aim's gone haywire, oh dear, 'tis clear.
I lob with great fervor, my aim takes a dive,
My own winter shot hits—can I still survive?

In frozen attire, I prance like a fool,
Declare myself king of this icy, cold pool.
Though victory beckons with a wink and a spin,
I wonder tomorrow if the snow will all win!

A Labyrinth of Winter's Breath

Snowflakes dance like little sprites,
But I can't see my own two feet!
A mitten here, a scarf out there,
Where did I put my winter seat?

The snowman grins with carrot nose,
While I slip slide, oh what a show!
My hot cocoa's gone and spilled,
Now it's a chilly, chocolaty glow!

Neighbors laugh, they watch me fall,
I try to wave, but I'm buried deep.
They build a fort, I build a wall,
Of fluffy snow in a tight heap!

So here I sit, embraced by white,
Thinking joy hides in every flake.
Tomorrow's sun might bring delight,
But for now, I'll catch this break!

Surrendering to the Storm's Fury

Why's the snow so deep, I plead?
I'm starting to think it's a trap!
A rabbit hole of frosty greed,
I guess it's time for a mid-nap!

With every gust, I think I'm lost,
Or maybe just discovering fun.
My sled's been claimed by winter's cost,
But hey, what's one more run to shun?

The neighborhood pets frolic around,
While I'm trudging like a clumsy bear.
They leap and bound, without a sound,
And I just hope I don't get stuck there!

So let the flakes continue to fall,
I'll wear this snow like a crown!
Embrace the whimsy, heed the call,
Of winter's giggle, not its frown!

Fragments of a Frozen Journey

I step outside, all bundled tight,
But who knew snow would fight back?
It swirls and sways, what a silly sight,
I lose my path, I can't keep track!

With every flake, my joy ignites,
Creating castles in the morn.
Amidst the chaos, laughter lights,
Even as my socks are worn!

A snowball flies, I try to duck,
But missed the mark, oh what a luck!
The chilly laughter fills the void,
As I become the winter's toy.

But listen closely, hear the cheer,
Winter's magic is all around.
I'll shake this snow as I persevere,
In this frosty playground I've found!

In the Grasp of Winter's Fury

Whirling winds that tease my hat,
I chase it down, into the fray.
But every gust sends me flat,
Flopping around like a ballet!

A snowdrift calls, "Come take a dive!"
So face-first I go, oh what a thrill.
Buried in fluff, I'm glad I'm alive,
Just me and this wintery hill!

Impromptu slip-and-slide, oh wow!
My friends gather round for some fun.
With every slip, we scream and bow,
It's true, winter's kooky, never done!

Yet soon the sun will shine so bright,
And melt the mischief we once knew.
I'll treasure these moments in frosty light,
With flurries of laughter, pure and true!

Echoes of Winter's Fury

Snowflakes pirouette like ballet stars,
Winds whisper secrets from afar.
Socks mismatched, I wear to survive,
Dancing with icicles, feeling alive.

Coffee's gone cold, I sip the frost,
Tracking my footsteps, but I've lost.
A snowman winks, says 'let's play!'
While I trip over driftwood, 'hey, hooray!'

My gloves are two sizes too big,
Waving to penguins, oh, what a gig!
Carrots for noses, those sneaky thieves,
Who knew winter could bring such mischief and eves?

But laughter echoes through the chill,
As I wobble down this frosty hill.
With tumbling snowballs, my aim's a mess,
Winter's wild antics, I must confess!

A Heart in the Frost's Veil.

Under blankets, I snuggle tight,
While frost paintings find their light.
Waking up feeling like a frosty cake,
Who's got the remote? Oh, for goodness' sake!

Hot cocoa spills down the side,
Did I bring marshmallows? Oh, I tried!
Snow morphs to forts, rivalries arise,
With laughter ringing, under icy skies.

The dog takes off, chased by snow,
While I'm stuck yelling, 'Where'd he go?'
Sleds are my steed, I zoom and I glide,
Till I tumble into a snowdrift's tide.

But with every slip and frosty fall,
I know this season's the best of all.
Heartbeats quicken with every freeze,
What a whimsical world, oh, if you please!

Whispers of Winter's Veil

Snowflakes giggle, a ticklish chill,
As frost creeps slyly, o'er the hill.
I stumble in boots that make me trip,
While squirrels conspire, they quietly quip.

Scarves wrapped tight, looking like a mummy,
Tripping on ice feels kinda funny.
With every adventure, blizzards we chase,
Yet footprints lead me to the wrong place.

The cat is a snowshoe, on a frosty quest,
While mittens get lost, in my funny vest.
Cocoa and laughter, what a delight!
As we celebrate winter, with all our might.

A snowball to dodge, then giggles erupt,
Life's a snow globe, and I'm all wrapped up.
This chilly chaos holds joy unconfined,
Winter's comical whimsently bind.

Frozen Echoes in the Gale

With flurries around, I strut with flair,
Stuck in my jacket that's two sizes rare.
Losing my scarf? What a tragedy here,
Wrapped up like a burrito, oh, the cheer!

Sliding on pathways, I dance like a fool,
It's a winter playground, who needs a pool?
Snowmen are judgmental, with brooms held high,
They nod like they know how cold can fly.

The wind whispers tales of castles so grand,
While I ask the pigeons to lend me a hand.
With snowball fights getting out of control,
Each icy throw aims for the heart and the soul.

But here in the bluster, fun takes the lead,
Each frosty misstep plants a joyful seed.
Let's toast to the winter, its quirky parade,
With laughter as soft as the snow we've made!

The Beauty of a Chilling Embrace

Snowflakes dance like playful sprites,
Hats fly off in wild delights.
Icicles hang like endless spears,
Winter's laughter drowns our fears.

Sleds crash down the hill with glee,
While snowmen scream, "It's cold!" "Not me!"
Footprints vanish in the frosty air,
We trip on snow—oh, what a dare!

Hot cocoa warms our frozen toes,
Marshmallows giggle, then they doze.
In this chill, we find our cheer,
Wearing frostbite like a souvenir!

Echoes of a Frigid Heart

Frosty whispers tickle my nose,
Socks are wet, and so are clothes!
The snowball fight goes on and on,
I can't see you—ah! Where has he gone?

Snowmen wink with carrot grins,
Laughing at our frosty sins.
The air is thick with snow and glee,
While penguins slide—wish it were me!

All bundled up like a marshmallow,
Sliding down, I feel so shallow.
Falling face-first, oh, what a sight!
Chilled is the heart filled with delight!

The Path Less Trod in Frost

On a path where no one dares,
I ski with flair and awkward flares.
Snowflakes tumble, a fluffy disguise,
I try to jump—oh, what a surprise!

The trees are draped in winter's cheer,
I shout and slip, but never fear.
A snow angel waves from the ground,
In silent laughter, joy abounds.

Hot soup waits at our cozy den,
We plot revenge out in the glen.
Bring on the cold, I'll face the chill,
Tomorrow's frolic awaits my will!

A Mosaic of White and Woe

Winter's canvas, white and bold,
Every flake a tale retold.
Socks mismatched, my toes are cold,
Yet charming moments never old.

Riding on a sleigh so fast,
In my mind, I'm built to last.
I hit a tree, not quite the plan,
But laughter echoes, yes, I can!

With friends we build a snowy fort,
In this chill, we often cavort.
But as I slip, they all just stand,
As winter's laughter takes command!

Whispers of the Snowstorm

As snowflakes dance like giggling sprites,
I trip on boots that slip and slide.
Each flurry giggles, a jolly sight,
As I tumble down with arms spread wide.

Hot cocoa dreams and marshmallow fights,
But icicles hang like daggers white.
I wave to the snowmen, they bring delights,
While my mittens take off in full flight!

Ice on my nose, it's quite the show,
I make a snow angel—oh what a view!
But my halo's crooked, like something from a crow,
Wishing my hair wasn't freezing too.

Yet laughter echoes, I'm not alone,
In this swirling world, we share our moans.
We ride the snowdrifts, like kings on thrones,
In this chilly summer, where winter's shown.

Chasing Flurries

With cheeks so rosy, and boots so tall,
I race the wind, try not to fall.
Snowflakes tease like a game of ball,
I throw a snowball—hit the neighbor's wall!

Giggles rise in the frosty air,
Snowmen wink as if they care.
My sled's a rocket, just a bit of flair,
And I'm the captain, without a pair!

Chasing flurries, I dive in deep,
Cold all around, but laughter I keep.
Each icy tumble makes my heart leap,
In this snowy chaos, I'll never sleep.

Candy cane dreams turn into a fright,
Snowballs bouncing, what a delight!
But watch out for my frosty bite,
Creating merry havoc in winter's night!

Beneath a Shroud of White

Under fluffy blankets of snowy delight,
I wear mismatched gloves that don't feel right.
I build a snow fort, prepare for a fight,
But the snowball hits me, oh what a sight!

Chasing my children in circles, we spin,
With noses all red, where do we begin?
Snow angels splatter, where I fit in,
And I laugh so hard, it's a win-win!

Frosty breath hanging like cotton candy,
We race the dog, who thinks it's dandy.
Mid-throw, my mittens feel quite handy,
But now I'm a snowman, looking quite sandy!

With branches for arms, I'm stuck in this pose,
As my family laughs, they act like pros.
With everyone's joy, winter nicely glows,
This snow-day magic, who really knows?

Frostbitten Memories

In the chill of the day, with a grin so wide,
I slip on ice and take a slide.
Oh, the frosty tales of warmth and pride,
As my friends roar laughter, they cannot hide.

With snowflakes kissing each rosy cheek,
I trip again, it's a weekly peek.
My dog thinks it's play, so spry and sleek,
But I'm arguing with snowmen, feeling meek.

Sledding down hills, oh what a thrill!
But my hat flies off as I laugh and spill.
We gather around, sharing stories at will,
Of every frosty mishap and funny chill.

Frostbitten memories fill the skies,
Laughter erupts, water from our eyes.
On this icy journey, under snow-draped highs,
We find joy in chaos, to no surprise!

The Weight of White Within

I bundled up like a walking coat,
With layers so thick, I resembled a goat.
Snowflakes play peek-a-boo on my nose,
While I trip over boots, oh how it shows.

My gloves are stuck, can't grasp the door,
I made a snowman, but now I want more.
He's got a carrot that's sad and drooped,
Guess he's not the only one feeling cooped.

Frosty cheeks and a silly grin,
I'll dance with snow, but where do I begin?
Each gust of wind makes my hat take flight,
I'm losing my sense, is it day or night?

Yet laughter bubbles up with each tumble,
In this frozen maze, I cannot grumble.
For at the end of this chilling spree,
I'll thaw out next to hot cocoa and glee.

A Hidden Journey through the Storm

The snow's a blanket, soft and white,
But I can't see past this frosty plight.
With every step, I lose my way,
Is it summer yet, or just another grey?

My nose is red, like a neon sign,
I can hear my toes scream, 'This ain't divine!'
A squirrel teases from a snow-laden branch,
While I fumble, trying to take a stance.

Once a proud adventurer full of zest,
Now I'm a snowball, with clothes in a mess.
I built a fort, a real work of art,
But I'm stuck inside; I don't know where to start.

Oh, the tales we'll tell of these snowy days!
Impromptu snow angels and icy ballet.
Though the weather's fierce, my spirit won't yield,
Join me for laughter, it's the best shield.

Tales of the Tenacious Traveler

With every flake that floats on by,
I ponder how to say goodbye.
To the warmth of home, oh so inviting,
Instead, I'm here, the snowflakes biting.

My legs are tired, and slipping is real,
With each little twist, I do a windmill reel.
The map is buried under two feet of snow,
Who knew the world could be less than a show?

A penguin slides past, with a winking grin,
I think he knows joy that I can't quite spin.
We share a chuckle, nature as our stage,
Two silly travelers, zero in rage.

In this winter wonder, I'll weave my tale,
Embrace the quirks, let my laughter sail.
For though I stumble in this frosty quest,
In snow and in fun, I find my zest!

Flickering Lights in the Frost

The lights above twinkle like stars that fell,
While I trip on my feet, oh do tell!
My scarf's on my head, oh what a sight,
Rearranging for warmth, I'm a disheveled knight.

With breath like smoke, I weave through the fluff,
And wonder, is this adventure too rough?
Snowballs fly by, friendly fire at play,
I duck like a ninja, then slip away.

The door to the cafe is partially closed,
I wipe my brow, and I feel exposed.
Hot coffee awaits, or maybe just tea,
But first, I must conquer this snowstorm spree.

So here's to the chaos, the laughter and fun,
In the grip of the chill, I'll never run.
With each frosty moment, let joy be the gust,
For out of pure madness, out springs my trust.

Embraced by the Frigid Night

Snowflakes dance and swirl about,
A frozen game of hide and shout.
I tripped on drifts that looked like hills,
Caught in laughter, dodging chills.

My scarf's now tangled, my boots a mess,
A snowman grinning, I must confess.
As I tumble into fluffy white,
Who knew cold could feel so light?

The wind it howls, a playful friend,
With icy fingers that twist and bend.
I chased my hat, it flew away,
What's lost in snow is here to stay!

Beneath this winter's frosty cloak,
I'll weave my tales, I'll laugh, I'll joke.
So here's to fun, in cold delight,
Embraced today by this frigid night.

A Memory Buried Beneath Snow

Woke up to white, what a surprise,
Snow piled high, reaching the skies.
Where did my garden go, I wonder,
All buried beneath winter's plunder?

The sled's my steed, I'm off with a cheer,
Down the hill, shouting, 'Whee!' in glee here.
I drop like a stone, face-first in the fluff,
This icy thrill, it's just enough!

Pockets full of snowballs, armed to the teeth,
I challenge my neighbor, a duel, a wreath.
Just when I think I'm winning grand,
He slips and falls—his plan's disbanded!

Laughter echoes in the chilly air,
Memories bloom in the cold, laid bare.
While winter reigns, I laugh and glow,
These moments are precious, 'neath layers of snow.

Whispers from the Icy Abyss

Huddled close in thick attire,
I hear the snowflakes softly conspire.
They drip and drop with teasing frost,
A balmy adventure, never lost.

I went for a hike, but who knew?
Each footstep muffled, stuck like glue.
I talked to a tree, it shivered in shock,
Its bark laughed back, like a ticking clock.

The neighbors built forts, oh what a sight,
With walls that lean, and goals in sight.
Snowballs fly like spaghetti tossed,
Victory's sweet, but who's really lost?

As night creeps in, a chilly throng,
I'll cozy up, where I belong.
With whispers of warmth in the freezing mist,
I chuckle at winter—never missed!

Reflections in a Winter's Dream

Mirrors of ice, they catch my fall,
I wiggle and tumble, what a brawl!
Caught in a moment, I fumble and sway,
This slick little dance dreams my day away.

Hot cocoa waits, my toasty prize,
I sip and shiver, with joy in my eyes.
Outside the window, the world's a play,
While I'm snug inside, I think I might stay!

Snowmen salute and birds wear hats,
I laugh at their style, give friendly spats.
The winter's embrace, oh what a game,
In this frosty world, nothing is the same.

So here I snuggle, with smiles to beam,
In this cozy nook, life's but a dream.
Let the snow fall thick, let the cold unfold,
In laughter and warmth, let adventure be told!

Surrendering to the Snowbound Night

A whiteout dance, so wild and free,
With snowmen prancing, oh what glee!
My scarf has gone, it took to flight,
Chasing snowflakes, what a sight!

The dog thinks he's a furry seal,
Pouncing through drifts, what a reel!
Hot cocoa drips on my warm chin,
As we brave this, let the fun begin!

The car is now a winter mound,
A snow fortress, cold all around.
But what's this? A sneaky snowball?
Friend or foe? I could take a fall!

Laughter echoes, muffled yet bright,
In this chilly, frosty night.
With every slip, I can't help but grin,
Let the snow games commence, bring it in!

Shadows at the Edge of Dusk

Snow shadows twist, the night grows bold,
Talons of frost, they grip and hold.
A squirrel notions, 'Hey, I'm here!'
Cheeks full of acorns, full of cheer!

The wind plays pranks through trees so bare,
It stole my hat, no shame, no care!
Downhill I tumble, a jolly roll,
Laughing so loud, I lose control!

Icicles dangle like frozen spears,
I pause to ponder, wipe my tears.
Oh, how slippery this crest can be,
Onward I go, it's fun, you see!

At night, we gather, hugs all around,
Mittens lost but laughter found.
Let frosty friends share this delight,
In shadows creeping, we'll stay bright!

In the Arms of the Arctic Night

Wrapped like a burrito, snug and tight,
I dream of summer in this snowy night.
Yet here I am, in fur-lined bliss,
Snowflakes tickling, I can't resist!

Time for a snowball, aim for a tree,
Oops, it hit Tim! What a sight to see!
Giggles erupt, we're a playful bunch,
Like penguins waddling out for lunch!

The moon's our guide, so hefty and round,
In this silvery glow, magic is found.
With every tumble, giggles ensue,
Made a snow angel—wait, what's that, too?

Layers of frost, we slip and we slide,
Joy in this chaos, along for the ride.
In the arms of winter, laughter prevails,
In snowy delight, we tell our tales!

Whirling Leaves of a Frozen Past

Whirling and swirling, what fun we find,
A slide of ice, and I'm intertwined!
With gloves in the air, I make my play,
As snowflakes twirl in their dodgy ballet.

Frosty whispers beckon me near,
Shadows dance while I hold back fear.
Will I stand still, or tumble again?
The laughter echoes—yes, let it reign!

A frozen past, where sights belong,
In each chilly breath, the fun grows strong.
Snowball fights spark laughter and cheer,
Winter's here to turn frowns to a sphere!

As night captures corners of fun around,
We shimmy and skate on this winter ground.
With memories built, we'll never feel frail,
In our icebound hearts, we shall prevail!

The Tempest's Tumultuous Heart

The wind howls loud and clear,
As snowflakes dance with cheer.
I trip on drifts, oh what a sight,
My dignity takes flight!

A snowman laughs, with carrot nose,
While I in mittens, lose my prose.
I chase my hat that twirls away,
And faceplant in a frosty fray!

The neighbors peek, they shake their heads,
"Might need a guide," they softly said.
But in this maze, I'll find my way,
With icy tales by end of day!

Oh, winter's prankster, full of fun,
Each slip and slide, a glorious run.
So here I stand, amid the white,
With laughter echoing through the night!

Trapped in a Flurry of Dreams

Snow clouds blanket the sky,
As my car drifts by and bye.
I wave to folks, they wave back too,
While I question just what to do!

The map's all fogged, a blurry sight,
I end up where there's no street light.
But wait! Is that a snowflake theme?
Or merely visions from a dream?

With frozen toes and jumbled thoughts,
I dance around in boots I've bought.
"Oh, look! A sled!" I yell with glee,
Then crash into a snow-topped tree!

At last the snow, it's my best friend,
With every tumble, curves and bends.
In this wild winter, fun's the claim,
No dull moment in this frosty game!

Echoes of a Softly Falling World

The snow whispers secrets low,
As snowballs fly to and fro.
A fluff of white, I try to catch,
And hit my friend, oh! What a match!

The drifts are deep, I search for clues,
While wearing mismatched winter shoes.
Each step I take, a squishy sound,
As giggles rise and joy abounds!

The frostbite grips my frozen nose,
As I look like a funny rose.
I pose for photos, all aglow,
With cheeks like apples wrapped in snow!

In winter's arms, I find my groove,
With clumsy leaps, I bust a move.
So let it snow, let laughter swell,
In frosty fun, all's well that sells!

Winter's Reluctant Embrace

The snowflakes fall like glittery stars,
But oh dear me, I've lost my car!
I search and sift through piles high,
While penguins laugh from passing by.

Hot cocoa spills, a comfy treat,
I wear the mug upon my feet.
Amid the joy, I trip and slide,
With snowflakes twirling in a glide!

The icicles drip, a winter tune,
As I try to dance beneath the moon.
But who am I, in snow so deep?
A jester caught in winter's sweep!

With cheeks all red and hair like frost,
I'll claim the fun, no laughter lost.
As snow men cheer and snowballs fly,
In winter's grasp, I'll always try!

Stranded Beneath Snowflakes

Flakes tumble down, a fluffy white maze,
Can't see my feet, I'm in a snow craze.
Got lost on the way to my car, oh dear,
My latte's gone cold, but I'm full of cheer.

Hats fly away, gloves dance around,
I trip on a mound, fall flat on the ground.
A snowman waves, he's quite unimpressed,
While I question my life choices, a jest at best.

Snowballs are flying, but I'm too slow,
A kid hits my back with a surprise throw.
I laugh at the chill, embracing the fun,
This wintery day can't be outdone.

With cheeks all aglow, and hair full of flakes,
I waddle like penguin, it's all for the laughs' stakes.
So here's to the snow, the cold, and the cheer,
Next time I'll bring a sled, let's keep this near.

The Cold's Grasp on Memory

My brain is frozen, can't think of a plan,
When did I last see my left winter span?
An icicle hangs like a sword on my head,
Lord, I should've listened, stay home instead!

Every corner I turn, there's a snowdrift tall,
Maybe I'll nap, this could be a ball.
Oops! There's a snowbank, waving salute,
I'm telling a snowman I'll clean up my boot.

The sled that I bought is now stuck on a tree,
Was it that high? It seems painful to me.
My hot cocoa's cold, what a dreadful fate,
But laughter and snowflakes, there's fun to create.

So I sip on my drink, watching kids play,
Who knew getting snowy could brighten the day?
Memories freeze in a humorous way,
Here's to hot cocoa and joyous dismay!

Wanderlust in a Wild Blizzard

Adventure awaits, or that's what I thought,
Stuck in this white stuff, oh boy, I was caught.
I'll ask for directions from a passing snow hare,
But he just looks back, with his fluffy white stare.

Footprints behind me, where did they go?
Each step feels like swimming through mountains of snow.
I finally spot shelter, oh what a relief,
But it's just a mirage from my snowy belief.

A snowball brigade thwarts my escape plan,
Kids all around me, do I even stand?
With laughter erupting, I just can't complain,
Who knew being buried in fun could be plain?

So here's to the chaos, and flurry of life,
Snowmen and laughter, and maybe some strife.
Let's dance in the flakes, stomp where we roam,
In winter's wild dance, I've finally found home.

Adrift in Frosty Veils

Cloaked in a shroud of frosty delight,
I'm on an adventure, or so it feels right.
Drifting like feathers, I can barely see,
Where the sidewalk ends, and the wild winds decree.

Can't tell if it's dusk or the dawn of my fate,
But I'm twirling with snowflakes, it's never too late.
An ice sculpture winks as I stumble past,
Is it me or does winter appear to be vast?

My phone's out of service, no maps can I find,
Guess I'll just follow the giggles behind.
An army of snowmen beckons with glee,
Who would've thought blizzards could turn out so free?

With cheeks rosy red and a heart full of light,
I'll embrace every flake till the end of the night.
So here's to the frost, and the friends that I make,
In the wild winter play, I'll never forsake.

Veiled in Winter's Grasp

The snowflakes danced, oh what a sight,
My hat flew off, what a funny plight!
Penguins around me, they laugh and slide,
While I tumble down, I can't seem to hide.

My gloves are soaked, my nose turns red,
I trip on drifts, I joke instead.
With snowmen grinning, their carrot noses,
I ponder life with frostbitten toes-es.

A snowball fight ensues, I take aim,
But a gust takes my shot; it's all quite the game!
My friends all chuckle, I'm caught in the fray,
I guess I'm just not built for this play.

So here I stand, a snow-covered fool,
With laughter around, it's the best kind of school.
Embracing the cold, I can't help but smile,
In this winter wonderland, let's stay for a while.

The Lament of the Wandering Mind

My thoughts are bundled in layers of fluff,
Where is my coffee? This snow is too tough!
I wandered 'round corners, oh where did I go?
Now I'm tracking my steps, but they hide in the snow.

The squirrels are scurrying, hoarding their loot,
While I'm debating, should I turn, should I scoot?
A snowman critiques me, he's got quite the view,
I laugh at his judgment and wonder what's true.

"Help! Where's the path?" I shout to the sky,
My boots are now heavy, the cold makes me cry.
Yet snowflakes keep falling, a comical plight,
I'll find my way home, after five more bites of light.

So here in this maze, I chuckle and prance,
With snow in my pockets, I'll take one more chance.
For in this odd journey, a smile I'll find,
In the topsy-turvy world of my wandering mind.

Spirals of Ice and Isolation

I twirled on the ice, it was fun for a bit,
Till I spun too fast, oh, what a misfit!
With graceful intent, I slipped on a patch,
And now I'm upended like a topsy-turvy match.

The trees are all quiet, the snow is a fluff,
But here's a lone snowman who's just a bit gruff.
"Hey, buddy! Smile big!" he seems to implore,
But my face is half buried in snow, oh the score!

I stumble on forward, the cold bites my toes,
Wondering just how all this madness arose.
With spirals of laughter, each step that I take,
It's a foolish endeavor, a delirious wake.

So when the skies clear, and the sun starts to shine,
I'll laugh with the snowmen, none of us pine.
For life's just a dance in this wintry play,
With spirals of ice leading me on my way.

Beneath the Weight of Snow

There's a blanket of white, and oh what a weight,
Like my pile of laundry, it just seals my fate!
I dig through the drifts, with each heavy shove,
Swearing next winter, I'll just hide in a glove!

My car's now a mountain of ice and despair,
Keys jingle like wind chimes, I'm gasping for air.
With a snow shovel ready, I think with a grin,
"How hard could it be? Just a notch and a spin!"

But the snow keeps on falling, my shovel grows tired,
While neighbors are laughing, it's me they've inspired.
We'll build a grand castle, oh what a delight,
And all from the weight that once put up a fight.

So beneath this cold cover, I'll find joy anew,
With friends by my side, we'll create quite the view.
For laughter's the warmth that will always suffice,
As we dance through the drifts, oh wouldn't that be nice!

Wandering Through White Shadows

White drifts are piling, oh what a sight,
I think I just saw a snowman take flight!
Chasing my gloves, they're dancing away,
Is this winter's game? Can I laugh or just sway?

With each step I'm sinking, a soft little groan,
Snowflakes decide they want me alone.
I twirl with a snowball, but miss my own hat,
Who knew winter hide-and-seek could be like that?

The world is a wonder, all wrapped up in white,
Yet I trip on my laces—oh, what a sight!
I wave to a snowman that winks in delight,
Imagine he's laughing; I swear it's just right.

So here's to the laughter beneath all this frost,
With a pop and a tumble, no moment is lost.
Through whimsy and laughter, I'll challenge the chill,
For within every stumble, the heart finds its thrill.

The Dance of Snowflakes and Silence

Snowflakes pirouette, a silent ballet,
But I'm caught in a flurry, oh what do I say?
With cheeks like tomatoes, my nose looks the part,
As I dive for my scarf, which is lost in the art.

The trees wear white hats; they look quite absurd,
I swear I heard one of them laugh, it was heard!
I step on a twig, it snaps like a joke,
Puffing out snow clouds, I'm now quite the bloke.

My boots are betraying, they squeak like a kid,
"Snow's not my friend!" I cry out and I skid.
A snowball appears, flying fast from the left,
I duck just in time, showing how I'm bereft!

Yet, under the cold, there's magic and glee,
Where laughter hides deep, and it's carefree.
So twirl with the flakes, let your worries be light,
In this snowy madness, there's joy in the fight.

Chasing the Ghosts of Frost

In a swirl of white, I chase frosty dreams,
But every ghost giggles, it seems!
They lead me in circles, a frosty parade,
With icicles dangling like charms that they made.

The trees are all grinning, a jolly old crew,
Waving goodbye as I tumble anew.
My mittens are damp, my socks filled with ice,
Handstands in snow? Now that sounds quite nice!

Oh look at that snowman! He's tipping his hat,
"Join us for snowball fights!" he says with a spat.
With laughter and snowflakes, I follow the cheer,
While shadows of frost dance, my vision is clear.

So I leap like a ninja through frosty delight,
Trading clumsy prances for snowballing bites.
With each laugh that rings, I'll continue the chase,
For within every ghost, there's a shimmer of grace.

Heartbeats in a Snowstorm

Flakes are swirling, like confetti they fall,
But I'm caught in a tumble; hey, isn't that my ball?
With cheeks all a-glow and a nose like a cherry,
I'm becoming a snowman; now isn't that merry?

The wind howls a tune, I think it's a song,
But I can't find the rhythm; it's all going wrong.
As I dance with the drifts, a dizzying ride,
Even my shadow is slipping and slide.

I giggle so hard, my knees start to quake,
And a snow angel's wings I suddenly make.
With laughter echoing through this snowy spree,
I chase after dreams that are wild and free.

So here's to the heartbeat of winter's embrace,
Each stumble and giggle, a joyous race!
In the storm, there's a pulse, a life full of fun,
Where laughter's the beacon and joy's just begun.

The Howling Wind's Lament

The wind sings loud with a chilling breath,
It twirls my hat off, a dance with death.
Snowflakes landing, they stick to my nose,
I swear they giggle, oh how this blows!

Icicles dangle like tiny swords,
Dangerous chandeliers, just my reward.
Slipping and sliding on sidewalks of ice,
I'm more like a penguin, but that's not nice!

Hot chocolate spills, my jacket's a mess,
Snowballs in battle? I must confess.
But every fall's followed by laughter's cheer,
In this frosty world, nothing's severe!

So bring on the winter, bring on the cold,
With icy adventures, let the fun unfold.
For every misstep in this snowy land,
I'll cherish each giggle, every slip of hand.

Echoes of a Frozen Dream

In a frozen land, the snowflakes twirl,
Slipping and sliding, what a wild whirl.
My gloves are soggy, my boots full of frost,
With every stumble, I feel I'm lost.

Snowmen are staring, judging my grace,
With carrot noses, wearing a face.
As I dive to dodge, I'm not so refined,
A snowball to the back, oh how I'm maligned!

Frosty breath dancing like ghosts all around,
I'm a comedy show, without a sound.
Each puff of white says, "Come take a look,"
As I waddle and waver, I should write a book!

Yet in every tumble, there's joy to be found,
Snow angels whispering, "Stay close to the ground."
A reminder that laughter's the key, my friend,
In a world turned snowy, where giggles don't end.

A Dance with Tempest

The blustery gusts make me question my fate,
Whirling around like a dizzying mate.
With boots like anchors, I try to progress,
But snowflakes conspire, leading to mess!

I twirl and I spin, a ballet of clums,
Each step I take, sound more like a thrum.
Meanwhile the snow laughs, seductive and sly,
Even birds above seem to giggle and fly!

My scarf's a wild creature, flapping in glee,
A flag of surrender, oh, woe is me!
I chase it down paths, through snowdrifts and glee,
Only to tumble and lose all my dignity!

Despite the cold rebel twisting my whiskers,
I dance with the tempest, laughter it whispers.
And though I may stumble through winter's cruel test,
Each frosty misstep is a joy I invest!

The Veil of Winter's Embrace

Veils of white cover the world so bleak,
Yet in this winter, the fun's at its peak.
I trip over snowbanks, oh what a sight,
I swear even snowmen laugh with delight!

The chill bites my cheeks, now rosy and round,
As mittens go missing, they've vanished, unbound.
Each slip on the ice, a graceful ballet,
An orchestra of giggles, showcasing my play!

The snowflakes conspire, for every soft fall,
A frosty reminder to humor it all.
While snowdrifts are dancing, I join in the fun,
For winter's a circus, and I'm the one!

As the sun peeks out, shining bright and clear,
I chuckle at chaos, there's nothing to fear.
For beneath this white blanket, with laughter we bask,
Each winter's embrace is an unasked, sweet task.

Milton Keynes UK
Ingram Content Group UK Ltd.
UKHW021939121124
451129UK00007B/152

9 789916 942864